HANUKKAH

Festivals and Holidays

By June Behrens

Photographs Compiled by Terry Behrens

 CHILDRENS PRESS, CHICAGO

TO DOROTHY LENDY

ACKNOWLEDGMENTS

The author wishes to acknowledge with thanks the assistance of Rabbi David Lieb of Temple Beth El in San Pedro, California and Rabbi Leon Kahane of Temple Menorah in Redondo Beach, California for their contributions to the preparation of the manuscript.

A special thanks to members of the Goldwasser family—Larry and Sharon, Michael and Michele, and Sam and Shirley.

Others who helped by serving as photographer models include Nina Uzick and Irv Chernik, and members of Rabbi David Lieb's family—Estelle, Amy, Jacob, and Adam.

PHOTO CREDITS

ELYN MARTON: Cover photographs
Selected scenes

DAVID TUCH: Western Wall, Israel, Page 7

Hebrew Union College Skirball Museum, Los Angeles:
"*A View of Solomon's Temple*," page 11
18th Century Engraving
Synagogue Scene, page 14
Charcoal drawing by Edward Cloyes Gorradbi (1830-1900)
Hanukkah Lamp, page 16 (photo at left)
Poland, 18th Century
Sabbath Lamp, page 13
Germany, 19th Century

Library of Congress Cataloging in Publication Data

Behrens, June.
   Hanukkah.

   (Other lands, other people)
   1. Hanukkah (Feast of lights)—Juvenile literature.
I. Behrens, Terry.   II. Title.   III. Series.
BM695.H3B43   1983   296.4'35   82-17890
ISBN 0-516-02386-1

HANUKKAH

HANUKKAH

A latke party! We're getting ready for a latke party! What a happy time of year this is. It is the festival of Hanukkah, a time for remembering a great victory and a miracle.

My father says a miracle is a wonderful happening, beyond the laws of nature. The miracle we celebrate at Hanukkah happened over two thousand years ago.

Hanukkah brings the family together. It is a time to sing and dance and see dear friends. Hanukkah is a time for giving gifts and playing games and eating special foods.

Mother makes potato latkes for the party. Latkes are potato pancakes served with sour cream. We'll have apple sauce and jelly-filled doughnuts called savganiot. And we'll drink all the cider we can hold!

Hanukkah is a religious holiday for our family. It is celebrated by Jews in every land. We are followers of Judaism. Judaism is the first religion with a belief in *one* God. It dates back more than three thousand years.

Jews live all over the world and are of many nationalities. We all have a common belief and history.

Hanukkah, sometimes spelled Chanukah, is a mid-winter festival. It is one of our happiest of holidays, lasting eight days. Mother and Father decorate our house and get ready for the twenty-fifth day of the Hebrew month of Kislev.

Kislev is the name of a month on the Hebrew calendar. The Hebrew calendar follows the moon, and is called the lunar calendar. The twenty-fifth day of Kislev might be in November one year and December another year on the lunar calendar we use. Our teacher, Rabbi Lieb, circles the date on our calendar.

The Hebrew word *hanukkah* means dedication, and the holiday is sometimes called the Feast of Dedication.

When we gather in our homes to celebrate Hanukkah, we dedicate ourselves to our faith and our God. Grandpa tells us about the miracle of the lamp. We hear again about the great victory won by our forefathers.

The victory was won for religious freedom over two thousand years ago. At that time the Jewish people of Palestine were ruled by King Antiochus of Syria. He tried to force the Jews to give up their faith. He wanted them to follow the teachings of the Greek religion and the Greek way of life.

We like to read the story about how the Jews refused to obey the king's orders. The king's soldiers attacked and captured the Jewish Temple in Jerusalem. They dedicated it to the Greek god Zeus.

For three years a small band of Jews, called the Maccabees, fought King Antiochus and his soldiers. At last they drove his powerful Syrian army out of their land. It was a great victory!

The Jews took back their Temple in Jerusalem on the twenty-fifth day of Kislev. They cleaned it and threw out the Greek statues. They made the Temple ready to dedicate to God in Heaven.

Father reads the part about Jews needing sacred oil for their dedication. The oil was used in a lamp called the Eternal Light. It burned twenty-four hours a day to remind people that God was always with them.

The Jews found just a few drops of
the special oil, hardly enough to burn
for one day. It would take them eight
days to make the new, pure oil needed
for the Temple dedication.

The Jews lit the Eternal Light, using
the little bit of oil they had. It burned
the first day. Then the second, and the
third. The special oil burned in the
Eternal Light for eight days. It did not
go out!

Father shows us a picture of the wise men in the Temple who lived so long ago. The men and their followers knew this was truly a miracle.

Today, over two thousand years later, we remember this miracle in the Temple of Jerusalem. We light candles every night for eight nights in our homes and synagogues.

Our Hanukkah week is a "Festival of Lights." We have Hanukkah lamps of many shapes and sizes in our home. They are a reminder of that miracle.

We all feel the excitement on the first day of Hanukkah. The holiday begins at sunset. All male members of our family wear yarmulkes, or skull caps, to show respect for God.

The Hanukkah lamp is a candlestick
with nine branches. There are holders
for eight candles, one for each day of
the Hanukkah celebration. The ninth
candleholder is for the servant candle,
called the Shammes. The Shammes is
used to light the eight candles.

SSShhhh. The candle-lighting
ceremony is about to begin. The sun
has set and we are ready to light the
first candle, on this twenty-fifth day of
Kislev.

Before we light the first candle with
the Shammes, our family says a
special prayer. As the candles glow, we
renew our faith in our God. We think
of Jews all over the world lighting
candles at this time. Each night, for
eight nights, we light another candle.

On the eighth night all of our family
gathers around. Grandpa and Grandma
join us as we light the eighth candle.
When all the candles are ablaze we
thank God for the miracles He
performed in times past and today.

When the candles burn down,
everyone joins in to sing a favorite
song, "Hanukkah, O Hanukkah." The
words in the song remind us again of
the miracle.

Now the latke party begins! Father
and Grandpa have a contest to see who
can eat the most of Mother's potato
pancakes. Later, we will play games
and sing our favorite songs.

Hanukkah is also the time for giving
presents. Sometimes we get a little
present for each night of Hanukkah.
Other times we might get one or two
big presents for the holiday. My
favorite Hanukkah gift is *gelt*. Gelt is a
gift of money.

Tonight Mother has planned a treasure hunt. Coins are hidden all over the house. We wonder who will find the first Hanukkah gelt.

Mother has invited friends to our party. We greet them with "Shalom!" Shalom is a word that may mean hello . . . or good-bye . . . or peace. Tonight it means peace. It is a warm welcome to our friends.

Our friends have brought a gift for
the family. It is a Mezuzah. Father puts
the Mezuzah on our doorpost. It is a
holder for a passage from the Bible . . .
the Torah. When people see our
Mezuzah, they will know this is a
Jewish home.

Mother has made all kinds of good
food. Besides potato pancakes, there
are delicious jelly doughnuts and butter
cookies. The table is full of holiday
treats.

After that last jelly doughnut, it's
time for *my* favorite song.

My Dreydl
O dreydl, dreydl, dreydl, with
    leg so short and thin,
O dreydl, dreydl, dreydl, it
    drops and then I win.

My dreydl's always playful, it
    loves to dance and spin.
A happy game of dreydl, come
    play, now let's begin.

Father made a large dreydl to decorate our house. It looks just like the little spinning top we play with. It has four sides and on each side is a Hebrew letter. The four Hebrew letters stand for "A great miracle happened there." Remember the miracle?

Time to spin the dreydl! Each of us puts a peanut in the "pot." Then we take turns spinning the dreydl. The four Hebrew letters on the sides of the dreydl also mean "nothing" . . . "all" . . . "half" . . . "put in."

The letter facing up when the dreydl stops tells the spinner what to do. After many spins all around, the person with all or most of the peanuts is the winner.

When the game gets exciting, the adults gather around to watch. This holiday of remembering and giving and singing and playing is our favorite!

Our synagogue has a special
Hanukkah celebration. The synagogue
is our house of worship. Some people
call it Temple. We come here to pray
and to learn more about our religion.

Rabbi Lieb, our teacher and leader, speaks to us from the Bimah. It is the raised platform in the synagogue. He reads from the Torah on the Sabbath. The Sabbath is observed from sunset Friday to Saturday evening. It is a day of rest and worship.

The Torah contains the first five
books of the Bible. It looks like a scroll
and is kept in a place called the Ark.
Rabbi Lieb opens the doors of the Ark
and tells us about the teachings in the
Torah.

Our synagogue is called Temple Beth
El. We have a large Hanukkah lamp in
the Temple. We sing joyful Hanukkah
songs and remember the words from
the Torah.

Our Temple is the center of Jewish
community life. In Sunday school
Rabbi Lieb tells us about the Shofar,
the Ram's Horn. It is used on another
Jewish holiday.

As we leave Temple Beth El after
Sunday school, we say good-bye to
our Rabbi. We wish him HAPPY
HANUKKAH! or say it in Hebrew...